Dinosaur School

DINOSAUR SHAPES

Please visit our website, www.garethstevens.com. For a free color catalog of all our high-quality books, call toll free 1-800-542-2595 or fax 1-877-542-2596.

Library of Congress Cataloging-in-Publication Data

Saviola, Ava.
Dinosaur shapes / Ava Saviola.
p. cm. — (Dinosaur school)
ISBN 978-1-4339-7148-8 (pbk.)
ISBN 978-1-4339-7149-5 (6-pack)
ISBN 978-1-4339-7147-1 (library binding) –
1. Shapes—Juvenile literature. 2. Dinosaurs—Juvenile literature. I. Title.
QA445.5.S33 2013
516'.15

2011048253

First Edition

Published in 2013 by
Gareth Stevens Publishing
111 East 14th Street, Suite 349
New York, NY 10003

Designer: Ben Gardner
Editor: Kerri O'Donnell

All illustrations by Planman Technologies

Printed in the United States of America

CPSIA compliance information: Batch #CS12GS: For further information contact Gareth Stevens, New York, New York at 1-800-542-2595.

Dinosaur Shapes

By Ava Saviola

I see shapes!

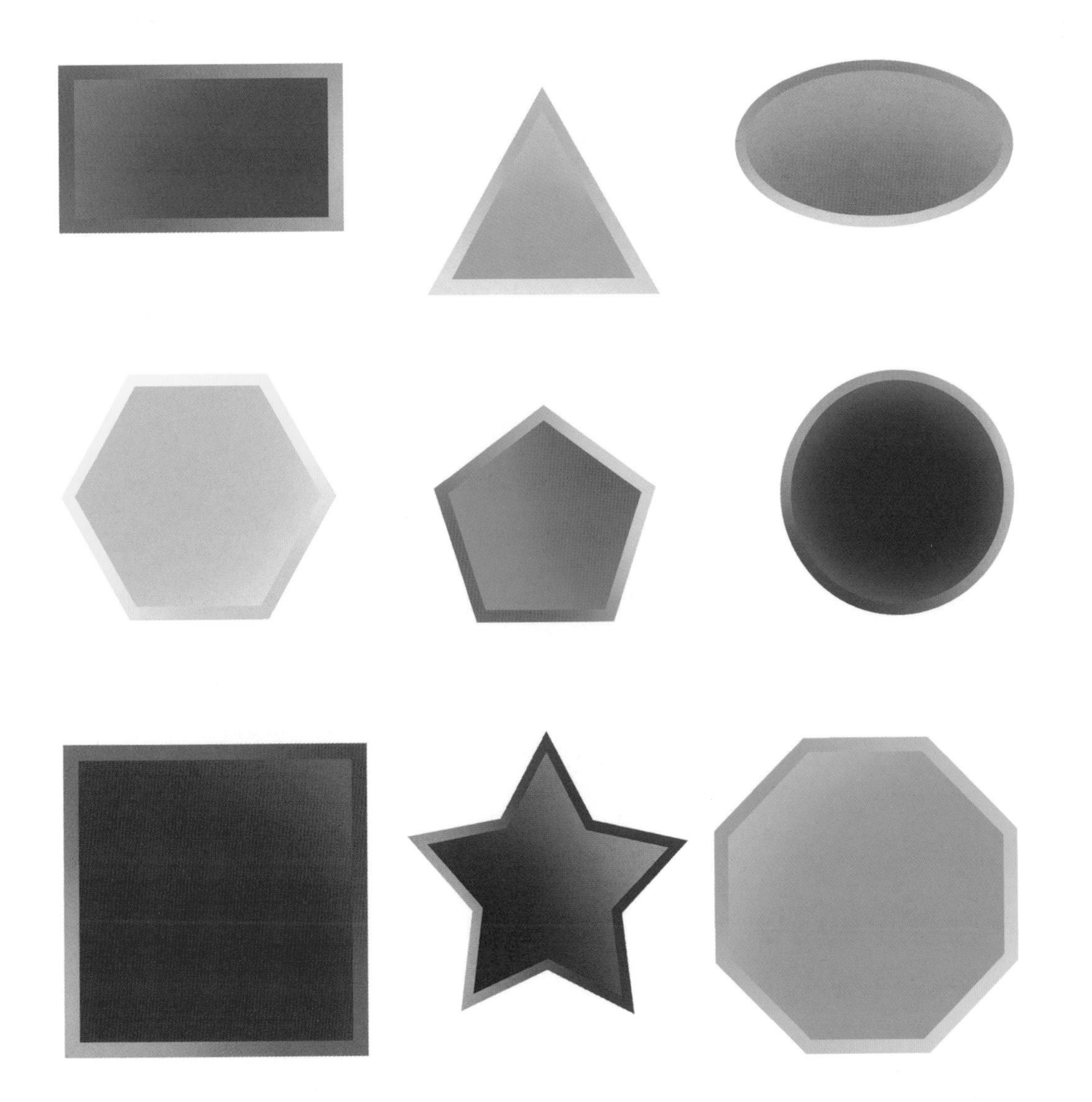

circle

I see a circle!

square

I see a square!

triangle

I see a triangle!

rectangle

I see a rectangle!

oval

I see an oval!

pentagon

I see a pentagon!

hexagon

I see a hexagon!

octagon

I see an octagon!

star

I see a star!

Dinosaur Shapes

circle

square

triangle

rectangle

oval

pentagon

hexagon

octagon

star